Traces of Presence

Traces of Presence

BETTY SPENCE

Negative Capability
PRESS
MOBILE, ALABAMA

ISBN 978-0942544-11-4
Library of Congress Control Number: 2014918964

Negative Capability Press
62 Ridgelawn Drive East
Mobile, Alabama 36608
(251) 591-2922

www.negativecapabilitypress.org
facebook.com/negativecapabilitypress

TABLE OF CONTENTS

UNCURTAINED WINDOW

SACRAMENTAL MOMENT

APPRECIATION OF ART DEEPENS WITH TIME

THE ROAD GOES EVER ON

ACKNOWLEDGEMENTS

UNCURTAINED WINDOW

Uncurtained Window

What-cheer, red feathers
dusting green feeder swinging
on black shepherd's hook.

Stitchery

as open and airy
as stanzas allowing
a sky blue canvas
to show through,
one evergreen stitch
at a time
Longleaf Pines
n e e d l e p o i n t
a piece of Alabama sky.

Taking Leave

(Old men ought to be explorers. T.S. Eliot*)*

How distant
the gaze of the old.
Holding a spread-out map
farther and farther away,
they see more clearly

where there is to get to.

Brown Leaf Dancing

(The fall of a leaf is a whisper to the living. Russian proverb)

Like any dry leaf
whirling its spiral down
to the leafy ground…
in your wildest
water oak dreams
did you ever picture this
reprieve,
halfway to your timely grave;
ever imagine a floating gossamer
might break your fall
and hold you aloft
for one last continuing pirouette;

or do I make too much of it?
But how often does one
like me
in her own front yard see
a viewless wire which by chance
has caught a leaf and let it dance
like wind and fire in a trance?

School Children View The Body
Of An 11-Year-Old Gang Member

The picture in the paper
shows them looking sideways
into the casket, mothers hovering.
Robert, better known as Yummy,
(he could live on animal crackers)
was to start sixth grade in the fall.
To find the hidden picture
look for a boy putting his tousled head
into the lion's mouth.

Call For Calendar Reform

Tell me Spring's not the time
to ring out the old; ring in the new.
Tell me the time of white blossoms
with a hint of pink is not the time
for bees to buzz the cup; not the time
for meadow grass to throw serpentine;
not the time for Yellow Jasmine
to trumpet strains of *Auld Lang Syne*.
Hey, you! You in the party hat.
Tell me the calendar didn't say that.

Laughing Gulls

(The poetry is in the redundancy. Donald Hall)

In clumps
of shoreline grass
laughter pips the shells
of three speckled,
sea green eggs
gently rocking
to raucous rounds of
Aha, haha; Aha, haha.

Rich In Sunrise

(In memory of Wallis N. Estill)

He amassed his wealth
panning for gold
settled at the heart
of sun streams
rivering
an Alabama sky
at first light.

Break The Wand, Break The Spell

A goldenrod
on a windowsill
leaves something unsaid
clearly heard in the clearing
where gone-wild flowers
cast a saffron glow.

Beaver Creek

All day and all night
it is in the background
of my listening and thinking...
there as I write or stoke
the woodstove or sleep
(dreaming) or make soup.
Often I peer out at it through
the window or step onto the deck
to listen to it, as if I need to check it.
I think it is myself I am checking.
Its flow is so like the flow
of my own living or writing—
slow and reflectively lazy
sometimes or full and fierce
in the rush of ideas and work.
It is my metaphor.
I am writing a stream.
I am living a creek.

A found Poem: *Breath for the Bones,*
"Reflections on Creativity and Faith" by Luci Shaw

On The Gulf Coast Midsummer
Is A Breeze

Come sit a spell where cedar shade
cools tombstones and enjoy the breeze
as it blows over broken angels
in Magnolia Cemetery. Even in the haze
of July, a soft, gentle wind lifts heat
off our clothes and off our bones,
sweeps oppression right out of our heads.

Our friends at Magnolia won't say,
but they remind us: We on the Gulf Coast
once loved the breeze. We timed our lives
around it, built our dog-trot houses
to catch it, dried our laundry in it.
We waited on the front porch for a blow
of good news like kids wait for Christmas.
We courted the breeze, danced it
like a lover in a midsummer's dream.

A found poem: *Garden & Home* column, Press-Register,
Bill Finch, July 13, 2012

Light Effects

Green-throated Sunbirds
perch on barren branches leafed
with Vermeer-like light.

No Such Thing?

Rainbow
of wood ducks swim
until a duckling grows tired
and jumps on its mother's back for a
free ride.

SACRAMENTAL MOMENT

Sacramental Moment

A spring or so ago I walked with Buechner
through a stand of maple trees at sugaring time.
If you were still, you could hear sap drip, drip
dripping into buckets hung out in early woods,
the sun coming down in long shafts.

The sap of a maple, he says, is like rainwater,
very soft and almost tasteless except
for the faintest tinge of sweetness to it,
and when I told him I'd never tried it,
he offered to give me a taste.

Unhooking a bucket from the tap,
he held it for me and when I bowed my head
to taste for the first time the life blood of a tree,
I had this feeling that he, of all people,
ought to be saying some words.

And for a moment unsaid benedictions
fell through the air like shafts of sun.
The whole place became another place
or became more deeply the place it truly was;
and he and I were awed with traces of presence.

A found poem: *A Room Called Remember*
by Frederick Buechner, writer and theologian

Come, Aeolian Breeze

(Psalm 137:2-3 NAS -New American Standard)

Come, Aeolian breeze,

> *By the rivers of Babylon,*
> *there we sat down and wept*
> *when we remembered Zion.*

Come, Aeolian breeze,
harpist, that you are,

> *Upon the willows*
> *in the midst of it*
> *we hung our harps.*

Come, Aeolian breeze,
harpist, that you are,
and strum the strings

> *For there our captors*
> *demanded of us song*
> *and our tormentors' mirth,*

Come, Aeolian breeze,
harpist, that you are,
and strum the strings
of the homeless heart saying,

> *Sing us one*
> *of the songs of Zion.*

Enoch's Crossing

(And Enoch walked with God: and he was not; for God took him. Genesis 5:24)

In step
with God, Enoch
never knew when the road
ran out and the bridge of faith locked
in place.

Unrecognized
(Luke 19:41-42)

Joshua Bell played incognito

and when he came near,

in a Washington subway on a January morning,

he beheld the city,

not many passersby, most of whom

and wept over it,

were on their way to work, stopped to listen

saying if you had known,

to the strains of Bach

the things which belong

rising from his Stradivarius.

unto thy peace!

When Joshua finished his music

but now they are hid from your eyes.

no one recognized him for who he was.

Source: Joshua Bell is one of the greatest violinists in the world.
See *Pearls Before Breakfast: Can one of the nation's great musicians
cut through the fog of a D.C. rush hour?* by Gene Weingarten in
the Washington Post (online) April 8, 2007.

Plotting The Resurrection

Old and too long, the Brooks' raincoat,
Seemed comical, yet there was something touching
about Katharine's gray appearance this fall day
when she got herself up for laying out
the spring bulb garden.

With diagram and clipboard in hand,
she waddled to the director's chair—
a folded canvas thing placed for her
at the edge of the plot where she sat
hour after hour, in wind and weather,
as Henry produced dozens of brown bags
full of new bulbs and a basketful
of old ones ready for the intricate interment.

Small, hunched over figure absorbed
in the implausible notion
there would, indeed, be another springtime
with its pinks and greens and yellows,
oblivious to the end of her own days,
she knew perfectly well was near at hand . . .
there she sat with her detailed chart
beneath dying October skies
plotting the resurrection.

A found poem: E.B. White's introduction to his wife's book,
"Onward and Upward in the Garden."

Wonder Of Wonders
(Psalm 88:12)

SHALL fireflies of intellect outshine
THY constant light, O Lord, or fantasies surpass
WONDERS of a stormy night?
BE unto us a jeweler's glass and make
KNOWN treasures of darkness
IN hidden places of the heart—
THE inner ranges where
DARK gems scintillate.

Grace Under Fire

Should I
lose heart grant me,
O Lord, the courage of
a tiger jumping through a ring
of fire.

Storming

(I will give you the treasures of darkness,
riches stored in secret place. Isaiah 45:3, NIV)

There is this
about pursuing
Presence—
you might just
find yourself
in that secret place
where storms
go to die.

Cradlesong

Let me hold him, Mary,
let one whose heart is all arms
hush-a-bye God's only Son.
Let me feign to quiet him
whose birth cry compels me
to cradle a baby born
to a mother having nowhere.

17th Century Pulpit Hourglass

Holding forth
on the evils of heresy,
blasphemy, and rebellion,
the ancient divine turns
the hourglass that tells
the not so-transient hour
and forthwith exhorts
his dead-to-the-world adherents,
every last one as solid as sleepers
the meeting house is built upon:

I know you are good fellows.
Prithee, stay and take
the other glass . . .
ahem, as I was about to say.

Hospital Volunteer

Wearing
a pink jacket
that barely covers wings,
she wears comfort shoes that glow in
the dark.

Tsunami Sounds Depths
Of Mother-love

In drowned-out villages
Indian mothers keeping vigil
for children taken too soon
from swollen breasts
pour pots of milk into the bay
to appease the Terrible Mother.

Trees And Folks

Last time
I was up this way
that tree was kind of
        drooping and discouraged.

Grown trees act
that way sometimes, same's folks;
then they'll put right to it,
strike their roots off into new ground
and start all over again
        with real good courage.

Ash trees are very likely
to have poor spells; jest ain't got
        the resolution of other trees.

There's sometimes a good, hearty tree
growin' right out of the bare rock,
out o' some crack that just holds the roots
right on the pitch o' one o' them bare,
stony hills where you can't seem to see
        a wheel-barrowful
o'good earth in a place,
but that tree'll keep a green top
        in the driest summer.

Lay your ear down to the ground
an' you'll hear a little stream
        runnin' runnin' runnin'.
Every such tree's got its own livin' spring;
and there's folk made to match 'em.

A Found Poem: *The Country of the Pointed Firs* by
Sarah Orne Jewett, (1849--1909)

31

God Remembers Noah—and Me

(I have set my rainbow in the clouds, and it will be the sign of the covenant between me and the earth. Genesis 9:13)

As present as sunlight
in the midst of rain,
as promising as green olive leaf
in the beak of a dove,
a prism casts a rainbow image
onto pages of Sunday's lesson
spread like bread
       on the kitchen table.

For God's Eyes Alone

(Roger Morigi was a master stone carver,
Washington National Cathedral, 1956-1978)

Scaling a scaffold
let down like a Jacob's
ladder leaning against
heaven's gate,
an artisan calls out to Morigi
who had spent days
chiseling leaves
in an all but hidden part
of a sacred tableau
as spirited as children
playing hide and seek:

Why is it taking you so long?
The leaves are beautiful.
But who will ever see them?

Wiregrass In Flower

Driven from that verdant, virgin land,
we must live knowing we might have
chosen innocence over encounter.
Nature has taken over; no longer
is everything lovely in the garden.
Yet, where fires of penitence
run rampant through thickets
that flower only when touched by flame,
world-weary grasses raise flags
as spirited as undulant fields of amber grain.

Street Preacher

Outdoor preacher, George Whitefield, 1714-1770,
helped spread the Great Awakening.

Unlike
the famed Whitefield
his voice does not carry,
yet the sight of him is hard not
to hear.

Poetics

(Now faith is being sure of what we
hope for and certain of what we do not see.
Hebrews 11:1 NIV)

Like faith,
poetry is
substance of things hoped for;
evidence of what is yet to
be seen.

Whispers In The Wind

(. . . *and after the fire a still small voice* -1 Kings 19:12)

It is the word spoken
beneath the breath—
the sigh you have to cup
your heart to hear
that quiets doubt and fear.

Sparrows Song

For all
the flightiness
of praying on the wing
I've yet to fly the notice of
God's eye.

Holy Hush

Just as
sound carries best
on a calm day, the still,
small voice speaks loudest to a heart
at rest.

Flower Child

In billowy skirt
she comes at dusk
to play guitar
and pass out Gospel tracts
outside the A&P.

Attuned
to *the heavens*
telling the glory of God
China asters,
break into pink and blue throws
so beautiful it hurts to look.

There! The sky! The sky!
Do you know the Lord?

*

On the darkening sidewalk
tired shoppers still with
the evening news to watch
avoid pain by not looking up.

APPRECIATION OF ART
DEEPENS WITH TIME

Appreciation Of Art Deepens
With Time

(Paul Cezanne, 1836-1906)

Critics of his day:
Imperfect talent.
Crude paintings.
No more than mere sketches—
an artist that never was.

*

Sister Wendy Beckett:
He wept over his struggles—
always felt himself to be
a failure. We could call it
the most magnificent
failure in art history.

Mulberry Tree In Autumn

Vincent Van Gogh—1889, oil on canvas

Sensibilities verging on madness,
he paints a tree growing up
out of rocky terrain outside his cell
at Saint-Remy, a Mulberry tree
whose leaves burn with autumnal fever.
His mind in a constant flux,
he paints not what is but what seems
in seeming swirls of yellow and orange that
dance canary with spritely fire and motion.
Art granting asylum, he paints
a tree that is a heap of gold
spun from straw, a tree that provides
warmth for the last of his winters,
a jeweled tree linking heaven and earth.

Note To Poetry
Contest Judge

As much as I would like you to sample
Persimmon Delight straightaway,
as one known to have a refined palate
for poetry, you know better than most,
ripeness is all.

I know when you touch ripe fruit
it will fall into your hand…and so on,
but the deadline is riper than the pudding
and I can only hope you haven't
sworn off persimmons for life.

Poet As Deep-Sea Diver

Unmindful of undertow,
with bated breath

she lets herself down
into cerulean upwellings.

O! the pull of a sea
that moves with such

a conscious air as this.

Marginalia

(For Nancy Compton Williams)

Poetic use of space
as white as conscious thought
illuminates her pages.
Wide margins make room
for unsparing commentary
on the largess of small
poems reluctant to reveal
all their beauty at once.

Third-grader's Found Poem

Don't worry about rules;
there aren't any, the teacher said.
Don't try too hard.
Poems are everywhere.

*

Walk with light...hmm.
"How did you come up with
such a beautiful thought, Julie?"
    "I found it on a traffic sign."

An Offering

(In memory of Roger Morigi, master stone carver at the
Washington National Cathedral from 1956-1978)

Scaling a scaffold
an artisan calls to one
long-since lost
in chiseling leaves
at a far remove…
never-to-wither leaves
that, for all you know,
could be health
for the nations:

Why is it taking you so long?
The leaves are beautiful.
But who will ever see them?

Wrist Slapped At Museum

(Pleasure is pure immersion. Susan Mitchell)

Plunging into
an acrylic seascape—
O! the pull that moves
with such a conscious air as this—

I finger-trace
cerulean brushstrokes
as viscous as honey set at flow,
but draw back sharply at:

"Pa-lease, do not touch the artwork, Ma'am."

God's Rock Garden

(After *The Story of Lighthouses* by Mary Ellen Chase)

But for cleft-nursed seeds
sown by families
of a lighthouse station
built on a rock island
off the coast of Maine—
a granite ledge
as bleak as ashes;
a field of infertile stones
drenched by dragon-like waves
giving rise to a beacon
flashing light as bright
as the face of summer's child,

but for handfuls of soil
brought from the mainland
and wedged into chinks
of slabby rocks as fixed as hope
firmly rooted in the human heart;
but for jeweled colors
of nasturtiums, zinnias,
carrots, lettuce, peas and beans
appearing at a distance to rise up
out of a formidable, gray sea,
Mount Desert Rock
would never have come to be called,
God's Rock Garden.

Ice Skater

(For Elvis Stojko, Olympic Ice and Figure Skater)

Always be like water
resounding in his ears,
fluid moves give a river
as breakable as bone
back its ebb and flow.

Silver-booted blades
scratch winter tracings
as fabulous as fishes caught
on alder limbs dropped into
holes in Walden's Pond

iced-over with magic panes.

Studying The Art Of Picking Blackberries

On the campus of a southern university,
a sudden start of summer rain
pushes me past a hillside in berry.
As if turning from green to red,
red to purple—black just like that…
and that just for me, blackberries
holler out: "Wade in and start picking."

Berrying is a matter of touch and take,
you know. At the slightest fingering
black satin berries sweetly let go.
With all the feelings of the body spreading
like wild fire to finger's tipmost ends,
without being taught, fingers know
when fruits of the earth are ripe.

Like William Stafford winching his way wildly
from impulse to impulse, passing himself
back and forth through the bramble-cure,
I follow the trailings-up; the climbings-down
of the Rubus, the Trivialis,
and find momentary stays purpling
on the ground beneath my feet.

Open Mike

Only in the company of poets
who in their own inimitable way
provide a listening presence,
do I really feel at home.

Reading my poems—
whoever finds the meaning
brings dessert next time,
is the price I pay
for community.

. . . fact, fancy, feeling—
a poem read to me
is a tasty casserole
I do not have to cook.

When nothing matters
so much as being there
for one another,
risking a quarrel
by sharing the stirring,
there's nothing like potluck.

Entry In Mary Oliver's Notebook

The line is the device upon which
the poem spins itself into being.
Verse, versus, *vers*, turn the plough,
turn the line. It is impossible to
measure the frustration I feel
when, after making careful decisions
about where the lines should turn,
an editor snaps off the long limbs to fit
some magazine's column-girth, or print-line.
Most especially in those instances,
when it seems inexplicable—
when the criminal act is accomplished
not by an editor but by a poet/editor.
To make a fuss to a friend is painful.
But I will fuss and fuss, and keep
the little leaping goat in his wide pasture.

Source: *The Poet's Notebook*, Edited by Stephen Kuusisto, Deborah Tall, David Weiss

Picture-taking At Malbis Memorial Church Where All Are Welcome To Rest, To Pray, Or Merely to Look

Twelve chandeliers as branched as cedars of Lebanon.
Ten massive pillars of red-streaked Parthenon marble
thrust upon ceilings as arched as a bow of promise
bridging a blue field of white and gold stars.

A dome rising like incense, a fresco of God
at its center, opening up that cerulean expanse
in which sun, moon, and stars illuminate
a threshold where boundaries dissolve.

Windows stained red, orange, yellow, green,
blue, indigo, and violet. Walls and ceilings covered
with murals and scenes from the life of Christ, portraits
of prophets, evangelists, apostles and martyrs.

Of all the pictures I took inside a rainbow,
the one that breathes life into them all
is of a lone man sitting on a pew looking up.

Source: *Malbis Memorial Church is a landmark Greek Orthodox Church of Byzantine architecture in Baldwin County, Al.*

The Legend of Itzhak Perlman

With measured step he walks from the wings
to his chair at center stage. Lays down
crutches, un-straps braces, pushes one foot back,
cradles his violin beneath his chin
and nods for the legend to begin.

Who's to say where in the score
a string b r e a k s? Who's to say
a violin concerto cannot be played
with three strings? Who's to say?

You always have your naysayers…
but I digress, he pauses,
shuts his eyes and begins where he left off…
changing   modulating   recomposing.

He raises his bow to quiet the crowd.
You know, he says, *sometimes it is the artist's task*
to find out how much music you can still make
                              with what you have left.

Yellow Brick Road

A lantern

The
Maker
Of haiku
Is wizard of
Ahs.

Fishing For Poems

Elisabeth Bishop's *The Fish*

Casting
a pulsing line
into an unseen realm
poets reel in *rainbows, rainbows,*
rainbows.

Chance Music

O the zing-zinging, the roll-rolling,
the rat-tatting, the hum-humming!

O the tink-tinkling, the trill-trilling,
the buzz-buzzing, the strum-strumming!

O the ping-pinging, the root-tooting,
the sing-singing, the drum-drumming!

O to come upon the Philharmonic warming up
in a scoop of summer woods behind your house!

Rooms By The Sea

(Oil on Canvas, Edward Hopper 1951)

I.

Like Hopper early at his window
watching a glory unravel at first light
(he had this early memory of gazing
at the house next door and sensing
a sort of elation about the sunlight
on the upper part of the house)
I watch the sun in its rising paint
my neighbor's east-facing house
with that, without which, there can be no art;
without which there can be no glory
moving through a sleeping house
turning on lights in every room.

II.

I've never summered at Truro on Cape Cod
nor been a guest at Edward and Jo's house by the sea,
but this visionary gleam conjured up
by a painter in a pensive mood receives me warmly
into a cottage perched like a bird reserve
on a sandy-cliff overlooking gray-green dune grass
which tries but sometimes fails to anchor shifting
sands to a restless sea awash with lapis blue
flowing from a full brush.

Poet As Surveyor

(The earth is the Lord's and the fullness thereof; the world, and they that dwell therein. Psalm 24:1)

Looking down from a mountain
boundaries and property lines
lose distinction, no sign
of Frost and his neighbor meeting
to walk the line/And set the wall between
them *once again.*
Looking through a surveyor's spirit glass
you know, *The earth is the LORD'S,
and the fullness thereof; the world and they
that dwell therein.*

THE ROAD GOES EVER ON

The Road Goes Ever On
(J.R.R. Tolkien)

Having nowhere, she laid
the more earnest claim
to easements granting
the right to come and go.

The Road goes on and on
Down from the door where it began.

On legs as long and black
as a wading bird's, she crossed
where no crossings are to peck
at stones that passed for bread.

Now far ahead the Road has gone,
And I must follow, if I can.

Walking perfectly in time
with music sounding in her ear,
kept her grounded… somewhere
up ahead there was to get to.

Pursing it with eager feet,
Until it joins some larger way
Where paths and errands meet.
And whither then? I cannot say.

Wheels Of Fire

(For Jim Ryun, Olympics Track and Field, Summer 1972)

For three minutes into the race
he is Achilles burning the wind,

every nerve one leap ahead
of a hissing at his earth-bound heels.

Then, with the suddenness
of a summer shower he collides

with another runner, is down
and 50 meters behind.

The gold no longer in it,
he rises in the sun of himself.

His very legs wheels of fire
warding off the coming cold,

he runs with the abandonment
of a two-wheeled chariot

rolling brightly down a hill
in some fabled summer festival.

Ghost Bike

The sun no longer moving
in its rounds to ward off
the cold, the poetry of motion
no longer rising and falling
to the rhythms of a musical journey,
pale blue forget-me-nots
spook their way in and out
of wheels no longer wheeling.

Reluctant Pallbearer

Stifled by strains of "Amazing Grace"
hanging like a pall in lily-scented air,
unwilling to lay wrong to rest—
all these years counting on just deserts,
it is his penance to celebrate the faith
of a scoundrel saved in nick of time.

Wouldn't you know with the Grim Reaper
breathing hellfire, and brimstone
down his neck, he would repent
and on his death-bed be baptized.
And wouldn't you know sweet Jesus
would forgive all such dying thieves

and wing them straight away to paradise.

Winter in the South

(A Kerf)

Raw January days
remind me of weathered books
too long neglected on some inner shelf.
With memory ablaze
I see myself beside brooks
reflecting the grand illusion of self.
Turning thus, leaf by leaf,
I am warmed by summers past
when no two days were ever quite the same.
Early buds stir belief
that coldness can never last
in a heart where hope is a hallowed flame.

Nothing Gold Can Stay

(After Robert Frost)

Every day now
the journey-bound hickory—
in flower before leafing out—
opens another, another
and yet another of its
gold-tasseled packages.

Playing pendulum
with catkins as tufted
as a young man's chin,
the gifted tree,
going green in its gold,
leaves me
to write thank-you notes.

Egg Candler's Daughter

Looking for shadows he hoped not to find, there was no poetry, no lore in holding on the slant the pointed end of egg after egg after egg over the glow of forty watts pushing its way up through a hole in the shiny lid of a *dis sho' am good* Uncle Remus syrup can.

When daddy set his mind to candling marketable commodities as fragile as an old man's bones, he was hardly distracted by notions of the world having been hatched from some cosmic egg or other. White was white: yolk was, well you know. Shells were shells and not containers for matter and thought.

He never once called out for me to look over his shoulder and see inside what let light in at every pore. But now as I let myself into a shadowy room called remember, a room smelling faintly of cinnamon and menthol, I watch as he anoints work-strutted hands with camphor oil.

Tripping the light fantastic, I see a philosopher gazing at candlelight without blinking. See fingers, fingernails, a palm glowing with the brilliant red glow of a neon lamp. See a hand throwing no shadows. A hand letting light in at every pore.

I close the door and smile to think that if ever an egg like a sun danced on jets of light passing through the Candler's hands, he was sure to have missed the show.

Stranglehold

An Alabama Pine, You Say?

The pine no longer answers to its name
or casts a proper shadow of itself
and though entangled roots imply an elf,
I, who should have known, am to blame.
You said the wistful vine would take the tree,
would curl like snakes around a magic wand,
but I thought it just the thing for a vagabond
who tramps about in search of poetry.
And even as you wrapped me round, you said
I was too much on passion and desire.
But what are words when feelings born of fire
fall like jewels from a dragon's head?

And even as I plant another vine
I catch a breath that is not fully mine.

Bag Lady Murdered In Lyon's Park

Just upped and moved at dead of night.
The Fox Squirrel holed up in the meanderings
of a Live Oak near the pavilion where she slept,
the only neighbor thought to see her go.

A perfectly good bedroll and shopping cart
pushed aside, everything just shrugged off
like a chrysalis… took her leave
with Mobile's pride azaleas still in pink.

Something must have come over her,
some sense of dread and foreboding;
some feeling of walls closing in; some
need to be freer than she had ever been.

Bearing Fruit In Old Age

(A Michener story retold)

One spring day a farmer
hammered eight, long,
and rusty nails
into the trunk of an apple-dumpling
tree no longer bearing fruit
with a star-shaped heart.

Prodded thus along, come autumn,
the old, abandoned tree
produced a bumper crop of blush-
red apples bigger and better than ever.

When asked what happened,
the farmer said:
"Hammerin' in the rusty nails
gave the tree a shock to remind it
that its job is to produce apples."

The Richer For It

(After May Sarton, *Coming Into Eighty*)

I think I shall live to be eighty-something—
I've seen how loath old poets are to leave.
Stick-figures in wind-puffed sleeves
staring down an ocean of words unsaid,
languishing for want of naming things
to others and themselves.

I've seen them piping like shore birds
on finding half-buried in the sand
a bottle thrown into a river at flood stage,
a bottle, for all I know, bearing the words:
Write the vision, and make it plain.

For all the times time has hurried me
I think I shall live to worry time along.
Already half-past the wakefulness of noon,
I'd like to live to sleep-in, sleep off poems,
live until lines in my face story forth,

live long enough to give away whatever
to whomever I please and be the richer for it.
I'll say goodbye but once—and that at the gate.
You can, if you like, watch me out of sight.

Love Apples

The winter of your dying past,
it's time to seed the tomatoes.
Looking in through a misty window
I find you in the greenhouse
pouring soil as sensuous
as any earthly delight
into rows of unsoiled foam cups.

With the firm hold
that bulldozed iron ore let go,
you touch an arthritic finger
to your tongue the better
to pick up and drop
into a womb-like cup
a seed that for all you know,
will produce summer flesh as
sweet as fabled apples of love.

Hope For the Homeless In The Lifted Cup

Out of time/out of place
he parades up and down
Dauphin Street
like a Mardi Gras reveler
trailing a goodwill blanket
as purple as a crocus
rushing to be first to celebrate
the lifted cup once frozen waters
thaw and start to flow.

To Everything There Is A Season

(Cover art—*Time of Singing*, Intermezzo, Fall, 2013)

A pumpkin-colored cover highlights
a cropped picture of a girl standing
beside a weathered park bench.

In her cream colored hand, she holds,
for all we know, Buscalgia's leaf named Freddie,
for whom *Spring had passed. So had summer;*

for whom living and lasting gave way to leaving.
But there, *asleep in the tree and the ground,*
were already plans for new leaves in the Spring.

Me Want It Now

(Playhouse marks grave of Nadine Earles, 1929-1933)

Earth-colored brick,
windows, awnings,
chimney, front porch—
lots of toys inside.

Little Nadine just couldn't wait
to play in the house
her father was building her
for Christmas.

Disengagement
Hourglass

She felt him leave
when they quit
sleeping
like
silver
wedding spoons
curve joining curve.

Myrtle And Me

Judson Jerome said if you knew Myrtle's poetry
you'd know her anywhere and there we were
on the same elevator on our way to an open mic
poetry reading in the Humanities Building
at the University of South Alabama.

Breaking the silence (poets are good at that)
Myrtle said: *"I'm, not a new wave,*
I'm kinda middle wave…
like, y'know, mainstream. It's high time
your garden variety poet got recognized."

Rising in apparent defiance of gravity,
it was the sheer weight of a satchel full
of purple passages Myrtle paid dearly
to have bound that grounded her (it's like
"ever' thing's heavier on your way up.)

And then, as if a fairy touched a button
with a wand, the door opened and Myrtle with
her satchel of fool's gold— and me, with mine,
stepped out onto a long green hall.

Barnyard Rembrandts

I watch him in an open field
braving winged thunderbolt,
watch him thrust a wand-like brush
into a bucket of white paint.

I pull off the road and watch
him paint a sign on a barn whose
boards are spirited with worm holes,
saw marks, checks and knots.

I watch him draw wayfinders
every bit as wonderful
as a child's free-hand drawing
of capital ABC letters.

Source: Clark Byers (1914-2004) painted hundreds of
signs on barns in southern rural landscapes advertising
Rock City Gardens in Chattanooga, TN.

ACKNOWLEDGEMENTS

Acknowledgments are made to the following publications:
Time of Singing
The Sampler
Avocet
Birmingham Art Journal
The Sampler, 2009
Harp-Strings Poetry Journal
Poem
The AlalitCom, 2014

A big thank you to Mavis Jarrell
for assistance and encouragement.

Praise for *Traces of Presence...*

Betty Spence has that rare ability to find the poetry in everyday objects and experience, and to elevate that everyday to a plainsong of joyous simplicity. Her poetry evokes the sentiments of Gerard Manley Hopkins, who asserts in "Pied Beauty" that "all things counter, original, spare, strange" are representations of the endless dimensions of creation, which should all be noted and celebrated. In Betty's hands, any moment may become poetry.

A perfect example of this skill is demonstrated in Betty's poem "The Legend of Itzhak Perlman" in which she describes the musician walking onto the stage to a chair at center stage, laying down his crutches and removing his braces before he tucks his violin underneath his chin and nods to the conductor. When his string breaks, he pauses, then begins where he left off, "changing, modulating, recomposing," recreating the music with his flawed instrument. When he is finished, he tells the crowd "sometimes it is the artist's task to find out how much music you can still make with what you have left." This metaphor for the human condition is deftly and delicately made, and it is this indefatigable attitude, this eye for the poetic moment, and this artistic dexterity that pervades Betty's work.

It is obvious from her poetry, however, that Betty's instrument is far from flawed, whether she is punning as in "Yellow Brick Road" when she describes the "Maker of haiku" as the "wizard of Ahs," or when she recounts a Michener story in the poem "Bearing Fruit in Old Age." In the later poem, a farmer "hammered eight, long, and rusty nails into the trunk of an apple-dumpling tree" which had stopped bearing fruit, because sometimes you have "to remind it that its job is to produce apples." In this poem, as in most of her poems, there is always more to the story than the story.

Throughout "Traces of Presence" it is obvious that Betty's job is to observe "all things counter, original, spare, strange" just like Gerard Manley Hopkins, to make music of whatever she has, like Itzhak Perlman, and in her own joyous way to remind us that poetry is around all of us everyday.

– P.T. Paul, author of *To Live and Write in Dixie*

ABOUT THE AUTHOR

As a mature student at the University of South Alabama, Betty Spence earned a B.A. degree in English with a concentration in Creative Writing in 1978. She finished post-graduate studies at USA and studied poetry writing with Dr. Sue Walker, Poet Laureate Emerita of Alabama.

From 1983-1995, Betty was a correspondent/photographer for the *Mobile Press Register*. For seven years she had a weekly column called "In the Neighborhood."

In 1988, Betty was a recipient of the Gayfer's Career Club's Outstanding Career Woman Award. In 1990, she received a resolution of commendation for outstanding professional achievement and community service by the State of Alabama House of Representatives.

Betty has had many poems published in a wide range of publications, both secular and religious. In 1990, she and Bettye K. Wray authored *Reading the Silences*, a chapbook of Pen Pal Poetry. In 2004, she published a poetry book entitled, "Pinned-on Wings."

Spence is a frequent winner in poetry contests and when she is not writing poetry, she writes *Life Related Learnings* for the Adult Sunday School quarterly published by Pathway Press. Over a period of several years, she wrote devotions for *Radiant Life* publications: *God's Word For Today* and *Take-Five Plus*.

Betty's memberships include the Alabama State Poetry Society (named Poet of Year, 1998), Alabama Writer's Conclave, The Pensters, a writing group, (former president). She served as president of the Mobile Branch of the Alabama Association of the National League of American Pen Women as well as president of the State Pen Women Association. She is a co-founder and facilitator of Greenleaf Writers' Group of Semmes, Alabama.

A native Mobilian, Betty lives in west Mobile with her son, Chuck.

www.ingramcontent.com/pod-product-compliance
Lightning Source LLC
Chambersburg PA
CBHW022035090426
42741CB00007B/1080